LIE AWAKE LAKE

LIE AWAKE LAKE

Beckian Fritz Goldberg

Oberlin College Press

http://www.oberlin.edu/ocpress

Grateful acknowledgment is made to the following publications, in
which some of these poems originally appeared: *Alaskan Quarterly
Review*: "My Zen," "Prologue as Part of the Body," "Question as
Part of the Body"; *The Autumn House Anthology*: "Back," "Fourth
Month," "Far Away Lake," "Wren"; *CutBank*: "Hallway"; *FIELD*:
"Answer," "One More," "Wren"; *The Gettysburg Review*: "Far
Away Lake," "Flying In," "The Week My Father Died"; *Gulf Coast
Review*: "Fetish"; *Hayden's Ferry Review*: "Back," "Lilies at
Night"; *The Journal*: "Eye," "List"; *The Los Angeles Review*:
"Curse"; *The Massachusetts Review*: "Open"; *Sou'wester*: "A Dog
Turns Back When You Turn Back," "Legend," "Tortoise"; *Swink*:
"Diving Horse Shuffle."

Library of Congress Cataloging-in-Publication Data

Goldberg, Beckian Fritz, 1954- .
    Lie Awake Lake / Beckian Fritz Goldberg.
    (The FIELD Poetry Series v. 18)
    I. Title.   II. Series.

LC: 2005922107
ISBN: 0-932440-25-8 (pbk.)

For Dick, for Mom, and in memory of Papa Bear—

Language continually regulates the appearance and disappearance of the human body.

—Elaine Scarry

The water never formed to mind or voice
Like a body wholly body.

—Wallace Stevens

Contents

1

2

3

4

1

Prologue as Part of the Body

It begins with something backward—
gardenia tucked behind
the ear as if scent could hear
its undoing

the fantastic bodice of a space
no larger than this plump
of sweetness, yeastlike, tropic

it begins with a turning, a trope,
that fragrance spiraling the cochlea
and the body confused by the enchantment
of the wrong orifice wrong passage—it was

after all where music should be unwinding,
cry shedding its epithelial layers, the tac-tac
of someone entreating, far away, some door...

But it was summer trying to enter, swoon its way
into the skull, the Parfum Fatale collapsing
on the organ of Corti

a secret island discovered by the Italian anatomist
of the last century though it was always there
in the body, the locus of quivering
like the letter M

deep in its alphabet, the humming
on either side. Beginning is

the flower to the ear
the flute to the palm, the glittering mirror to
the back of the head, the steaming rice and the plums
in honey

to the feet, to the vertebrae, to the pineal gland:

oblivion, oblivion, oblivion.

Eye

It was not by accident the eye
was attracted to the water,
the eater of doubles: the good
cattail and the bad cattail, one
rising from the other like the memory—the gnat
and the gnat, the sycamore reaching up
to heaven and the sycamore hanging down
to that heaven . . . So the dizziness
that beauty is, losing
is. And with this bark-colored eye,
this eye that was a father's and
a mother's, I drank
back the helpless world—the one
that is all body, not spirit, not
a bit—that is silt, sex, and germ
and the Temple of Being Beside. I was
young beside you, water, and my father and I
were on your face, there were willows, and this
was in early summer or at least
it has become early summer,
that double of once.

Flying In

Here I am, the last
place on earth . . .

The city has everything. It has

more windows
with more lights on
in them

than any
homecoming.

Father,
you're the far away lake

the far away lake

the lie awake lake.

Open

In the city of it
how soon grief
becomes exhaustion—

buildings pain-high
sheening like lead in the March sun,
here

and there, a crust of snow.
Sometimes in the middle of dinner
I want to go to sleep.
Sometimes

in the middle of this
white, white, separating rose
I have to
shut my eyes—
unearthly civilization—

the fumes, the radios, the nervous
buses, the man at the pay phone
shouting, So you're leaving me—

hates me for hearing—
but once

the wound is open, it all
must go that way . . .

One More

Say I had
a calf
I had to guide through the city,

old snow
in the curbs and fresh
nakedness on the branches
of each

fenced-off tree along
the avenues, black man
repeating to no one, everyone,
You got a problem?

You got a problem?
Leading a dewy-eyed young
calf through the traffic,
bastards

staring into its
lake-silt eye, one

then the other,
isn't a cakewalk, isn't
a walk in the park, isn't going
anywhere

among the strange bawling
of cars, water-trucks,
horns. Here,

say to it, say to it,
one more look.

One more look and
we must go.

List

It was all new.
One day I bought birds-of-paradise.
One day I cleaned the oven.
One day I made a list.
The next

I did the list.
One day I sat out and watched
yellow burrs fall from
the sweet acacias.
I did

all the being you
I could, father,

all the rest
of this life.

The Week My Father Died

My brother, drunk, said
always remember

the day you were announced
we were putting up
a corn crib from Sears Roebuck,

Dad, me, your sister was helping,
your brother was helping
but mother

mother was sitting
and dad told us

you were coming
it was autumn then
always remember

it was a happy day.
But

this day, this day,
sick with grief
and mean-drunk, my brother said then:

Look in my eyes, look,
what do you see?

Death, I thought, but didn't say.

I'm dying, he said. You'll
never see me again.

But it was the drink talking.
It was the torn heart saying
both things. Lies, lies . . .

Lies to remember.
Lies to make time even

Lies to get time
even with us.

The Railing

On the road to the city
rows of brown houses
rows of brick   each brick
bearing the weight of another
and then

balconies
and someone's railing hung with
old teakettles
I don't know how I got here

I don't know

how precisely your absence gets me
to this

to get back is all

I want—
it's a whole city
black windows and dogs and

a sheer whistle
the pitch   between lips . . .

Wren

Once I fished a wren
from the pool
held it

little volt
in my hand

This I won't forget:

my mother's shoulders

I'm in the backseat
holding my brother's hand

my sister is driving

I don't have to see
anyone's face

the box of ashes
queerly heavy
like metal

like
the soaked sleeve of your sweater

long ago

the way something would rather drown
than trust

the hand that would lift it

Answer

Yes, I'd go back—

to the day
I was almost born
to the false alarm

that brought a cop
to the motel room
to wake my father

and to the night drive
through the spring snowfall

black outside
a little blue light on the dash

but it was Not
Yet—

it was Too Soon—

I was born in May,
but I would leave them there

with the breath and the April snow
with the waiting
with the beginning

my happiness
so great
I'd never come . . .

Question

What is the moment
of greatest happiness?

And what if it's
behind you?

And thank God the mind
wanders. And thank your
lucky stars

you can live
without answers

but not without
stars   without
all of this outside you
all of this beside you

all spilled all
broken all swept—

And if you could stop time
and if all water were the stillest water
and if all light were the constantest

light and if
the flesh did not forget us
but it does forget us

it
the only moment

and it forgets

Far Away Lake

We can't get there
by road, by rope, by
wing

by time—
though time would be the way

by boat
by please please

time would be the way

then the reed-quiver
a cloud of gnats
mumbling its hypnotic suggestion

by sleep, sleep
until you say
lift my elbow   straighten
my legs

And I
straightened you in this life
like flowers

but the little water
there was
went to air
where it came from

And all my love for you
came back—
you couldn't take it where
you were going

you'd get halfway there
and then you'd drift
arms by your side

like a clock
plucked . . .

2

Question As Part of the Body

The essential question—
what do we ache for, what do we need, how do we get it?

or re-phrased: How do we not die?

How do we not see question as
part of the body?

Pain as. Light as.

Let's say the leaf is my body, the shoe
is my body, the city at night. And this might
lead me on

where are you is a part of my body, where are you
and where are you, my father, where are you,
where is that time
you and the lake and the willow and the bright
aluminum band of the car in the distance, or is
time that part of

my little finger I can cut off, I can jab with a needle
and squeeze . . .

There is a duct in the heart named
for the man who found it, and the crypts of Lieberkuhn,
after another man

but not even the roses of the nipples have the name of
    a woman,
and why?

And where are we women then when death
wants to call us in the flesh?

Answer wants no part of this—this

is no discussion this is the eternal
nag of the soul which is not

a ruby or a fork or a fawn
but a car caught in the distance
gleaming as if it were a moment, why

not confuse distance with time, time
with location, location with mass, mass
with energy energy with heat and heat, heat
with the body which wanders itself
pinching and parting & asking not *what am I* but
am I?

and what is more furious than rubies,
and what is more than the deer who bend
drinking themselves up from themselves wavering
there at the edge of light
and load . . .

Fetish

. . . a fetish is a story
masquerading as an object
—Robert J. Stoller

In ballet the foot disappears
and even the swan walks on air.

In this marvelous disguise of the body,
deception and beauty weigh

equally. Form is no dance,
though looking is, the leap

from here to
light's pink shrined upon the stage

while the music shivers. It's some winter, this
story of the foot

that later, through the stage door, walks away
in its black stiletto

the clarinetist behind watches disappear like a smaller
and smaller and smaller black champagne glass,

the mournful little toasts of desire over
and then that spectacle of bondage

as her strapped ankle withdraws into a taxi.
If this were the fairy tale,

the shoe would be in his hand, her shape—
and the shoe would be glass so that

her shape would seem to walk on air.
He'd name her Farewell.

But he'd keep her in a closet, he'd keep
for himself that image of the five red

half-moons of the toes, cozy and lingual.
He'd let that heel grind into

his breastbone, and why not, just think
of what we'll stand for in the name of love,

just think what we'll become a street for,
or a giving earth, a meadow for, a mud,

a heart-rooted grass. Think what we'll
disappear for in all our flesh, just to know

the gravity of our desire which is
always walking out, out, into distance

and then, when there's nothing
more, drawing itself up and lasting

a brief second like a circus goat
climbing a ladder, pitiable

miracle, our love, our art.

Lilies at Night

Surprise, they say in the dark.

And nothing happens.

Gazers, these
animals who sleep upright,

wax still, the wine red beauty-mark
here and there—
but so much shadow

and nothing.

Nothing wants
to be the body anymore.
Everything wants to be the soul
but something has to stay

something has to be the body.
These—

but open—
like blows in the side
glow of the kitchen,

and the eyelash, the anther, the red
vibrissa,

out
like the lamps extinguished in milk,
and the corpse swearing *I will not drink urine,*
I will not eat excrement,
I will be young . . .

Flower. Ear-mouth. Flower.
Foot-palm. Flower. Navel-eye.
Flower. Cock-heart.

Back

The god of the back
must be a lonely god,
god in the shape of man-headed hawk.

Long ago
a man had been sailing the river
and the hawk had been flying beside him
for days. Mornings,

the man would wake and look,
yes, there it was, dark tip-to-tip, the hawk.
His hawk, he began to think of it.
And after a time

he forgot the point of the journey,
he only woke each morning to see
if the hawk was there, to move if the hawk
moved with him, to not rest

if the hawk did not rest. And all of this love
was done in silence, between animal
and animal. There

beside him in the air and there
beside him in the water, the yoke
of the hawk. Once he had a family. Once
he had a city to go to and something

to bring back. More and more
he began to see his life
as a story the hawk was telling

holding the rat of the field in its claw, meaning
There is another world

and I will take you in it.
This

is when he became the god,
god of the back, the beautiful
brow of leaving.

Curse

Because it starts
without the body
without thought, the tongue

is a dangerous weasel,
because it thrusts
from one mouth
to another

though it can't swim,
it's a bad fish,
though it's golden

and flips
for any mere syllable
like a girl. Because it's an eel

the drudge-like heart loved
before they had words. Because

a woman kept a ruby under it
in the fairy tale

and the mortician stole it
when she died

and he gave it to his lover
who, when the mortician died,
tossed it in the lake

and so as the story goes,
the tongue goes,

because it's a glutton for going,
it doesn't want to be alone,

it wants to be bathed in salt
and it's also a baby
for sugar

it's just a naughty sea-slug after all,
though who hasn't wanted to slay it

because it slips. Because we should have
our eye in our mouth or our ear
or even the navel, some

sensible part that wouldn't
betray us
and be us—

perfidious cock.

Blood

Supernatural
red shadow
cast by some immense leaf
or wing, it began drifting
in the morning like the wrong
thought—a darkness
mapped to glow.

Death parts her hair, this
place on a woman
where everyone goes in
and is not heard from again.

The clouds are heavier than blossoms.
Spring paces.
I hear an airplane buzz roundly
into the grave sky, into
the reverse world.

At night, blood
won't shut its mouth.
The starlings return and knock
the window outside
from inside where their moon is.

Like them I am astounded off the body.

Yet I hold his head while he cries
between my still
swollen breasts
for what is about to happen
what will never happen.

Glistening, we
have never seen so much of our own.

Tortoise

When the tortoise came
to live in the water behind
the house, we understood
this as necessity.

At night, constellations lived there too.
By day, the acacia, the airplane.

Sometimes
dreams are kind
and we forget the life

in which we search for meaning.
We live
and let live, as the proverb goes.

When he came from the water
he was slicked dark
and dumb—dome and penitent—

The grass
and the trees were just like
our grass, our trees.
The air was just the air

I'd spoken to in sadder moments.
To live
on earth
you need to believe in

an earth
an ugly soul can come back to
having forgotten
the hell of form.

My Zen

One night the stars fall open—
in them bottomless doe-eyed topaz
and a floating meadow.

I am not on fire.
I am quite the ordinary December night.
The desert is clear, cars trail off mid-thought . . .

A meadow I swear is only a place
which you expect across—

something bounding, something coming, something
hopestruck.

In my childhood there was a cardboard house
whose windows opened like books—
and behind each, something

wrong, silly, like a fish or a cello
instead of a lamp or a chair. This is
what I saw—

one night there were stars and the moment
they came open, these whole atomic
lilies, petals where the arms of eons
rest . . .

They were only stars, mysteries, immortals, gas . . .
As if you could follow happiness to the end
of the world and not see where it goes.

3

Legend

When the river had risen
to the green glimpse it stole from land,
they did the work. The world began
with destruction, not creation.
They chopped up the body
and dumped it in the water.
They dumped it in the sand.
They scattered it on hills
over short blunt bushes.
What does it matter if they were
people or gods?
It remained for one
who loved the body to wander
the earth in search of the pieces.

This is how I came to the desert
gulch of owl's clover and bearded penstemon,
the lake of flowers.
I was looking for a mouth.

But all the blossoms were open
and little saucers of the dark had landed
in them. A dark wet cough of violet
sat on the horizon. Idiot spirit,
what do you want
but an arm and leg? Old
body-money.

This is how I stood, knowing
the first step out of the world is the last:
I was looking for a true rose,
for strong teeth, for that tongue
asleep

to turn.

A Dog Turns Back When You Turn Back

The desert won't get off my back
not even here in the green heart of Italy.
All night I lie awake and the cuckoos
repeat from the lindens repeat
the hours reliving themselves.
Then I lie on my back with

the desert beneath me.
My very gravity I feel depends
on this—cool wind, a flock of pansies
lighting in the window box, a flock of inks,
a flock of backward looks
you won't forget. I know

you can live in two places at once:
Whenever I go to bed the desert's there.
I say, "I thought I left you, I thought
we had it out." The desert
hardly stirs. My leg in the sheets—
the rustle of lizard
and no breeze: No matter which way

I turn, the desert stretches out,
content. I say, "Goodbye."
I say, "I don't love you."
And the whole pillow exhales its
creosote, its turpentine bush,
and even moonlight full of
strange silhouettes and valleys.
I blame my eyes, and roll onto
my side and stick out
my elbow just for spite. But

you know the desert doesn't budge,
lies like a drunk who hasn't shaved,
who can't remember where he went
or how, and drinks to not

remembering—a little birthday
eternally when the sun comes up.
When the sun comes up I open one eye
and, since it's still there, flat
and littered with arms of chainfruit cholla,
"I hate you, I hate you,"
I say and nothing listens. Of course,
nothing. Though the quail
go strolling the dry arroyo down
to the bedpost. I blame
my breastbone. I blame my ear.
I blame the globe mallow
and the city of rock squirrels.
Cursed, I begin to sing.

The song goes "Here, here
where the sea got up and left
I lie down." I blame my skin,
dry and withered and,
at that moment when the desert
drifts off into dream, I put
my hand into the blank space
beside me: out from it go
rings of terrible childhood, Sundays
in the white glare of gravel and
dusts, a brand of endlessness
I both fear and crave in large

doses—the result of this lullaby,
this thing near death
beside me, clatter of mesquite pods
falling on one another
and the sound of paper,
the sound of shore, the song of
what was the song . . .

that lovers and ex-lovers ask
when they try to go back—
Nothing follows *them* around, no
scorpion waiting in their shoes,
no mean little needles pricking

through their clothes. "Leave me
alone, leave me alone," I cry
as if I were not already

thirsty and desolate. Blaming
my feet. Blaming my tongue.
Love is never, no matter how many times
we say it will be, any different.
I come from a brutal unbearable place
and every time, even in the trees
and grapevines terraced
in the valley, the desert sits on my chest
and begins to beat.

Fourth Month

Finally, my father's soul came
to rest in the closet.
This is where you want
the dead—out of sight

and within scolding distance.
By now, it was June.
The grass shrank
and whitened. The sun,

the sun, was out every day
until we thought
it would never go . . .

Soon the nights would be still
and pointless,
too hot for bedsheets.
You want to sleep in air,
you want to sleep in water.

But what you feel is the sheen
of grief
like a sweat.

My aunt telling my mother
she should bring his ashes home,
to the lake where he was born,

my mother asking me is it all right
to wait—

but dear god who am I?

Nude Shuffle

nipples the light pins up to the bone

the lake of the rib below

monk of the body among desert thorns and brush

struck in dawn

the nude doesn't belong to the creosote

but a little to the chuparosa, thin red sockets

the ache of the ribs below

palm fronds shining like sweat

the common rabbit carries a little dirt for prayer

the seam of the buttocks, the book of shadow

what is the body doing letting itself go

the nude like a viol in a grove of piccolos and snares

oh lord an instrument is a cunning thing

long delta of the back, the buried pelvic girdle

the nude comes down the javelina path from the civilized road

I have been up all night and now the frightening sifts of gold

oh lord a light is a cunning thing

what is the naked creature creeping down the dry wash

sending out four coyotes on Thanksgiving day

right past the dining room window

named Death, Hunger, Hair, and Saliva

gambel quail beginning to bottleneck the green fountain

the house came with last summer

we threw out years and photographs and clothes and books

but look the house was haunted

Real Ghost

She thinks she lives
like anyone else

listening for a voice
looking for

those eyes—but this
is the story of water, water

and the cloud and the bird in it
which are also time
and time . . .

Yes, her hair
can rise, fan out
and her legs can kick

I can always do that—

There on the white edge,
the date palm with its claw
beside him,

everything echoing, gleaming
like cement

and over and over
he throws her in

and she swims to him
even as she writes this

the third person

she swims

Like This

You were wrong, you can't find the missing
leg or mouth or finger or eye or breast,
not here by the ocotillo or the blue torch,
the mounds where the gophers have tunnelled
under the prickly pear, leaving its bruised pads,
its rotted edges, though that other body might
be with you, phantom, as if you had eaten it and
then began your vigil of regret.
                              Or, as we would say
in the vernacular, the farewell has so fucked you up
you see it everywhere, you see yourself
from a distance, bending to kiss your father
above his left breast. Not thinking then, why this,
why not his cheek, his forehead, he was tucked in bed,
naked, confused about who should turn on the lights,
though it was daylight.
                          His legs had gone
long ago, though he used to dream, he said, of a black
horse named Nancy, who kicked in the stalls, kicked
in the door of the market. And he'd smile with admiration.
The next year God started on his spine. And you began
to see that any god would have to
hate the body, so transparent were its motives,
so transparent was its hope. Or, in other words, such
a mess of need and shit and swelling and shrinking
that it was a wonder it could bear itself.
                                    It could not.
These were the last days though you never know them
until after. They smelled of stale smoke inside the van
that took him back and forth to the doctor. It was an entire
day's work, getting him out of the bed, onto the gurney,
getting the gurney through the narrow hall and foyer of that house,
lifting it into the van, it took the four of you, and then later,
in the clean lobby, you stood with your father lying there
as if in bed, there in front of everyone staring and then
you got to wait, wait until the doctor had time. Wait, staring
at his bare shoulders while he asked where's my wife?

Then the doctor asked him what year it was, his name,
could he *go like this* and she bared her teeth and he bared his teeth
and he knew the year, he knew his name. The next day
he died. And the doctor was surprised as if it were some
bastard miracle, the soul saying *can you go like this* and the body
going like this.
                    But before that,
before that, after you explained the lights
didn't have to be on, it was afternoon, and he drank his juice and
you put down the cup, you leaned and kissed him on the chest,
and then you went. The breast and the breastbone
vanished. And the warm curve of his skull you used to put your hand on
and scratch his head. And then, though you were middle aged,
the girl-body disappeared completely—there was nothing to keep her.
You cut your hair. And won't go looking. You're sure the only
thing left is breath, the animal breath. At night you lie awake and
listen. It crawls up and curls on your stomach
and with both hands you feel its ribs swell out and out. And that's
enough for now. For *now* is the word of the body.

Hand and Cradle

When the hand begins to fly
it's awkward
and it cannot lift from
its earth, the body.
It can't be alone

and so like a shadow
is always depending.

At night, tucking up
the thumb in a fist beneath
the pillow,
half-mother, half-father

or sometimes leaving open
its emptiness like a cradle.
Next thing,

spring is crying out,
the nervous wet light . . .
and what is touch then but
the constant
tight chain that jerks us back,

that won't allow
the hand to leave the body completely
for another, but keeps it
always for its own end

and to itself like a dumb soul, so
if there is a heaven it's a heaven
only of returning—

the winged dark habit of the hand
whose song is nothing whose wings
are cups and latches.

Tortoise Return

This time the tortoise swam deep below
the surface, easily as shadow
slips a field—

shape alone, it glided the water
underworld. Across the pool

old sumacs and a metal
fence stood looking down, vibration
only—

Like dream, water made everything
bend, and I lay swaying
before myself

late February, almost spring.
Some things are made
to return and return and return

and we to remember
what can't. The tortoise's body stealthing
like a silk saucer

the floor of the pool, a dark jade

ghost with his brain pulled
deep in his breast.

God Body

At night he lay awake and listened to
the body, first the neck with its venous hum
its simmering monarchs of the pulse and then
oh the little rhoncus of the chest, those wings
stopped up in the lungs, the rub of plates and
the lubb-dupp of the heart. It was a jungle in there.
Not a garden. Not the beautiful fountain and
gentle thumbing of the leaves, but a hot
and saturated place, a terrible kudzu of passageways,
intercessions, and muck. In this first

tender auscultation, he was repulsed. How
was he going to go on? How to create desire?
In this first hour the whole skin smelled
like the washings of a gun. And great
microbial swarms threatened to steal it all.
But he couldn't go back to the beginning—
that was the tragedy of genesis, that was
the tragedy of desire, that was the tragedy
of body

so he kept it going. Swamp and all. He'd invent
everything to hurt or feed it. Even the little
stones to torment the kidney, or the mosquito
to fever it, or the shit of the rat to keep
the virus nearby when it slept. It was all
good, he told himself. Look at the hair, look
at the breath coming out like a lotus

listen to the bruits of the belly and the lowing
bowel. You can picture a field in all this.
You can picture a cupboard of fresh linens.
And the secret pouches of lavender . . .

Mimesis as Part of the Body

We are what we repeat
like the breath itself an ocean
the eye itself a fish,
the belly—soup
brought to its first bubble,
the clear omphalos.
Mine repeating you over
and over, the heart
beating up through the sex,
each step, each bump,
each fall like the last,
body of leaves, body of no mercy,
the breast repeating itself
and the sternum a pond
where shadow repeats its lips, oh,
love is everywhere, isn't it?
The guitar is everywhere, isn't it,
the moon and the wrinkled purse
the fig drops once in childhood,
seven times in memory,
a sickly droning of the blood
when a child puts her fingers
in her ears at night
and vows to stay
the way she is forever . . .

Speculum

To throw light in every hole of the body,
and to see for oneself, one's self, the wet
and opulent places, the labial curtains and the bright

blue neck of the uterus, the little stirrup of the ear,
the smallest bone we know. The pink bell
hung dumb in the throat. The living
tapestry of the sphincter, hungry and sick, hungry and
sick. The most glorious spot

on the wings of ducks, the teal
speculum, is that spyglass out
of the other living thing, the dint of beauty.
A look is a wound, it either brings the blade in
or rips it out.

The blue sheen that grazed off
the lake when I was standing there,
years ago, came with me. Came with me.

But my father did not come with me.
Yes he did.
I don't know where I see him, if it is
in the body, if the mind is part. He called me
on the telephone, *If you die in dream then
it's only a dream and then I can't really
be dead,* he said.

He sounded so happy I thought
I should go to his house and see if he's there.

So I created the house so I could see.
In his room he was lying down with blue blankets.
I looked and couldn't say
if he was asleep or truly dead. I woke
too soon to tell . . .

To look in and see the face of my father asleep,
to know it is there in the book of me,
in the same place and in the same word
when I fall open.

4

For myself, I would like a death that would give me more loves, not fewer. And greater desire, not less.

—Galway Kinnell

Blossom at the End of the Body

Leaving this world must be the flower,
its three violet faces turned to the air—a man can't look
at a flower without knowing he's dying.
That's the beauty. Parting must be this little
chance, with its stem and flutter. It's no god
and it's no force and our grief is a rock, a clod,
a punk of earth. Truth is,
what we will miss most
isn't her or him or mother or child but
the particular blue at the side of the field,
the heart's pure botany, for

the body is a science. And there is no
substitute for *thing*. Not love, not happiness,
not faith. But flower. But flower. But flower.

Purgative

I ate petal by petal, hip by hip, the whole rose,
blossom to burn out pain,
clarity by clarity the grouse's egg,
circle to pour out melancholy,
hair by hair the turnip's foot
to expel the humors. I drank
milk from old silver to loosen
stubborn love and broodiness,
electuary of hempseed to cure *déjà vu*,
boat by boat the bitter almond,
meat to push out disagreeable matters,
cheek by cheek the green muskmelon to move
the sanguine and the fecal demons
then—girl by girl the whole damned twelfth
and thirteenth years, the music teachers and
the sad walks home, heart
by knife by sip by tent by starry, I swallowed
elder sap and pollen
to evacuate the body and know
the vacuum of heaven and begin
to scat out birds of paradise and pure
oases and surely, somewhere,
a soul:

And then I drove
the desert highway great with low
constellations
and the thrill of emptiness sheering in
the lights and those moments when
the mind leaves the hands on the wheel
and hums to itself such songs, songs, not one,
not one about the past . . .

(brother leaning over the chair, father
standing by the willow, the blue iced
cake in the middle of the lacy table)
You divine yourself over and over

on the way home, late February, the desert already
believing in spring. Night roads,
who doesn't love them? Who
doesn't begin to dissolve on the moment
compatible and tuned,
the lark of the curve, the reflective sign,
the ordinary Sunday night and Monday
a holiday—

Chewed
eucalyptus bark to chase all measuring,
the powder of lizard's ash to flush away
misery, greed, nostalgia and *philosophia perennis*,
What is there ever to do but mourn time
with the next, last with the never,
shoulder with the breast, belly with the ankle,
talk to the night because every life comes
to this, the cloved onion slick
in its bedclothes entering the mouth,
fish oil to pass through the body its
ruminations and gall,
blossom to burn out pain
and all its juices—
finger by finger the aromatic buddha's hand,
rind of the rumpled citron riding to its humble
excretion, the scarab rolling its golden apple,
all down the river of body, all marsh flies
and accidental lozenges, all pornography and sleeps—
all wilt, all rot, return, & heave,
the undammed mercy outing flesh.

Hallway

In the dream you meet the house
and whisper
melodies are like this
the leaves turn the shower
of green, your mirror is drawn
and the backsilver
tightens: bride you are, and
bride you will be
my fleeting fleeting
shoeshine of earth—
door to door to window
you go, the gentians each
with their hallway lights
mother of the house
is your next step, breath
on it like a
single wing that takes
a slug of the transparent
as you leave the house
for a bed heavy
as a bag of honey.

Reliquary

The lid sighed backward
it was a perfect fit
with the scent of laburnum and saints
as if the box, open,
addressed the physical world
the box being a snapdragon
in the hands
of the blossom thief: the boy in
the hands of a future
looking inside
what if he saw tonight
the firecracker thrown in the corner store
busting open a box of chili powder
smoke and red dust
and suddenly we're all breathing in
desire and repulsion
because the open takes
something from us, but
Mr. Eros, you
ain't got a finger to stand on
not like a female saint
whose thumb is a shrine,
upright and petrified and guarded
by glass, permanently
testing the inner
atmosphere.

Sly Sparrow

What they sewed me up with would dissolve
that's what they said when they stitched my breast
over the heart the cat wouldn't eat
though she'd swallow even the bones. Now
I like to study
my scar in the face of the rain puddle
not as clear
anymore as when they shaved me
the better to graft my new wing, smear
my eye with emerald jelly. That's when
I was the cooperative sparrow. Call me
Jane. But when the thread
disappeared into me like a childhood
I began to call up song like a knot.
I became one mean musical
motherfucking sparrow: Call me Nicole. Though
by nature
we are a tolerant sort, like therapists
or pears. It's when I died I became
fierce and also I missed
the leaves, those only earthly
things that used to flutter under my weight
like eyelash over dream. Those nights
I drank I couldn't stop drinking until
I gave the thirst away to anyone
in need of a thirst from God.

Emily Dickinson Blues

Memory. . . .
Is eternally pink.
            —Dickinson

And in the late trees the leaves balance.
The cigarette pulls its ruby—

toward the mouth of the upturned spigot
propped on Emily's stone. Seconds

unworm the smoke. The doing
nothing till the break-apart bodices

fall. I want
only one day when everyone bakes bread.
The clouds are white as thistle, as

Assumed. Beside the shrine of cigarette
someone's left a pink bouquet, someone's
torn from a garden—

We want the dead to be like us
when they are not even like themselves.
But I want only the dead brain

of the Thumb pushing into the white dough,
its spiral face, the kitchen beyond
                    the moon's pan—

pink flowers still fresh in their wilt
wet in their fragile minds. A wisp

of smoke burlesques and—Disappears.
The petals a face of mouths.

The gravestone says *Called Back.*
In the light the granite's glitter and stain.

Why choose such a parse of Providence
to believe—and photograph the grave—Then

who have we met? to whom were we speaking?
What the hell do we know. Glitter and stain.

You'd think at least a poet had a spirit
as a leaf has ribs. And in the cool air birdsong

heavy as a season that way, a north
and an east of here where we need

the interruption of the present: brown birds
and the plumshock of dusk's

first angle. The dead are a small landscape,
plot after plot of a single crop—

and in the late birds black hearts float.
Sky bites its diamonds. At least

a poet has the desert, a desk with a snapshot
of a grave, the impromptu

tribute left by someone with smokes on them
and who stole the windflowers. As if

spirit had a nose. As if the dead have
a place. Here

it's windless, the cold trance of February.
But a dog can run beside it in

the meadow of another year. Beside
the white skirt . . .

We want the dead to be like us
who were never like us.

Risen, and cooled.

La Belle

Under the moon
the eye of the lake is open, white
and pupil: One or the other
must lose. Then it will mean
to be the book that keeps us
up all night turning
its pages. You can't sign
your name in this one
because at some point the book
becomes a mirror again
and the breath, a moon
from your lips. Don't despair.
Light is coming. Light is always
coming from a distant heavenly
death. Its fall broken now
by water, as a man, a moon,
disturbed by the deer's goodnight
kiss.

The name of the lake is La Belle,
where I drowned once. Stood
under the water with my brother,
a silver gaggle of bubbles
rushing from his lips. The rest
was slow and beautiful—the nether
horizon maned with blue
like a burning stick: Down
of the light coming. Moon
down rolling like a catseye . . .

Here Is a Good One

Desire walks into a bar.
The bartender says
What'll you have?

I'll have whole silken mounds of it,
cunning, baffling winedrops of it, cups
and bowls and vats of it
crushed, steaming, burnt or unburnt,
I will have its butters and spices and rosemary,
I'll have butterflies in my fists,
a pair of brief
averted glances. If they serve
anything in the afterlife, let it
be this—cherry as big as the moon,
for craving comes from the soul, not
flesh. And the soul wants to eat.
It did not choose to be this way—
In death, gluttonous, bottomless
like time . . .

The punchline is desire
never walks back out
like loneliness at Christmas.
It stays in the smoke and the glamorous
neon dropping pure pink on the window
with a heart rhythm
as steady as a hand—
to catch the figment, ripe.

An Underworld Primer: The Heart

Icon: Wood

What will happen if you tell all you know?

The heart does not presume an audience.

On the first day of school the souls face the chalkboard.
"Because," the teacher says, waving his pointer, "tongue
is nearly all muscle like the heart, human beings can swallow
water standing on their heads."

Is a heart a heart if no one listens?

The heart doesn't live in a forest.

"Each hour the heart throws out more
 blood than the weight of a man," says teacher.

The heart is merely a question: Why
did my father die? Not that the heart
didn't know death comes for everyone.
The heart knew. Every tree in the forest.

Icon: Glass

Fear feeds you faster than love tonight
while this night is tied to your window like a boat,
or your window is the boat and may
any minute break away . . . What speech
things are to one another

nothing is saying. I think the heart is the man
looking out the window during his honeymoon.

Why did he die? Why live if the end was always
here? But now

someone is strolling in his boots right down
the stream, gathering rushes, on some
murmuring television in the room where
I sit and write

to you, in the heart-moon.

Icon: Feather

Do you swear not to testify against me,
heart that was from my mother and father?

I swear.

Icon: Light

Did you honor the transparent?

I saw light in the flags of fish.

Did you count silences along with marriage proposals?

Officially, 118.

You forget the betrayals of love.
You remember standing in the kitchen the night he died.
You remember the light gleaming in the sink.

You recite your question: Why did he die?
How is he gone?

No such thing as overkill: a police car
outside the house
because he'd died at home, the blue
revolving lights. The death-fish
around the eaves . . .

Icon: Shovel

The shovel dove in just under my heart.
I must have been ice
to cling to it once
before it rested on the belly of the shovel
like a bloated radish. I must have been
lamp to see its hut, and the swim of the table
that never swims except in a ray . . .

And once I reached under my own
breastbone and scooped it out, laid
the heart next to me on the night table.
I was calm, glad I could breathe
without it. Then an angel came
with a plastic sack to freeze it for me.

The teacher says, "The heart is simply
a pump."

The pupils nod like undersea flowers.

Icon: Fire

*Is love erased? Does it last? How does everything
become nothing?*

Study stellar explosions.

Tonight, my sister says, is the last
night to see the Leonids in our lifetime.
So, I step outside at midnight
and look east: The three stars of the Dipper
bright and big as the handwriting
of girls who dot their i's with circles,
and the only light descending is a plane.

What part of the body truly holds us?

I am tired of being the one
carved on trees with your initials, the one
burning held out by Christ, the one the guilty
hear beating beneath the floorboards—

Our father, who was paralyzed, used to
fall asleep near the fire and not feel
the burns open on his skin,
and so the police would question us
that night

which wasn't their night. That, at least,
the heart held up as fact,

red, divine, and able to repeat
the beating mind of time
in the carpeted hallway as they carried
the body bag on the gurney . . .

Icon: Seed

Did you grow tired of love? I asked.
Heart replied, Yes, and loved again.

In an ancient now lost city,
they harvested the sylphium plant,
sweet fennel, to extinction—and with it
vanished all the city's wealth.

But what remains here and there
in the fields is their coins,
stamped with the earliest image
of what we call the heart, those two
even halves

simply the face
of the sylphium seed pod
which had brought the city
its greatness, ancient coins of Cyrene

for sweet flavors and midwives' cures,
ancient coins for love . . .

"The heart weighs five to seven pounds
and is the size of a fist," lies the teacher,
"And the right side is larger than the left."

The boy cuts
into the body on his table and
pins the skin aside to watch
the amphibian heart contract. Its
belly looks like an eyelid turned
inside out. He wants to put his finger
on that life, but the girl

is looking and he feels the look
all over him, the blue serene scrutiny
before cruelty decides.

Flame

The flame. Tell me how to get it
that lives by changing.
But it has hundreds of bodies.
It can't help its selves:
the room, the sun, the clear
solitaire of alcohol. The first
seabreeze that hits you like a nibble.
The sea. Tell me how to get it.
The sea, the sea, longing and longing
to drag some meaning into its life.
And here I sit opposite.
Here, I occupy. The bliss
is all we want and I'm
personally waiting for my Godshot.
The flame with its chugalug of blue—
I will settle for the miracle of the first
dusk car cruising the street,
of a red car smart as a daytime candle,
the one I lit for forgetfulness. The second
gust that sweeps you awake:
Am I dreaming or am I talking to someone?
For you must stay awake, be vigilant, be
extravagantly vigilant. How many lives had
you been living? The room, the sun,
the beautiful bottle, a window all
to yourself. You did not choose
the demon, but you shrewdly
chose the form in which he came.

Skate

The bed is a beautiful lie.
It believes you. You who were never
more relentlessly you. As l love
coming home late when it's still.
Even later, a man on a skateboard
sails down the middle of the street,
the only sound. Life
is this way. By some grace
you are not one of *them*. That
alone. You are a staying-
in-place. Stubborn as ugliness.
At night the sea is a lie—
it's only the sound of blackness
falling and falling and overripe.
As l hear the skateboard wheels
sh-thunk sh-thunk along the street.
A tide of sorts, but human. If I spend
my life praying to nothing what is lost?

Diving Horse Shuffle

and juggling dogs, he said, what do you think

the sun was out with mountains holding up his tail

she was thinking

at the point where our joy is greatest why don't we die

the doctor suggested animal therapy

the couch was orange as a cigarette

she was thinking

why doesn't he swing me from his trapeze

I think dogs can't juggle, she said

the sun began to slouch, losing his tail in the horizon

he was thinking

she was in love with the doctor whatsisname

like a potato in chowder

the couch was orange as a fist

why not celebrate everything she said swirling an olive

gin is the first law of gravity

look, my therapy is barking, she said

no, I mean instead of balls we juggle dogs

shit she was thinking

the orange was very much in love

the sun flopped down anywhere

here's to Fruit Loops, she said, I could suck them all night

he took out an anti-gravity Marlboro and lit up

goddam doctor

Christ awful couch

do you juggle them by their heads or their bottoms, she said

orange has no pity

"Look a firework shows/ its claws raking empty space:/
     and the wound is gold!"—*Basho*

Basho was a great poet

like a dragon is a poet

Basho was a great poet because he never wrote these words

she was thinking, why don't we die at the moment—

the couch was a juice stain in the middle of the room

Sex in Heaven

It was like two curtains touching,
essential curtains, filmy and white.
They took me back to a window,
a particular one in memory—
you can't look in a window and not
see it—not have desire
stare back like a parting,
the gold slit through the night.
Which body to kiss with? Which age?
The curtains were willing.
That's all it took to unlock the house
from our past and the past
that was better. For we were
paradisiacal creatures—and will
create it everywhere. Oblivion's
no different: you're born
longing for home. First, it's a body.
Or before that, the body's scent.
Then it's a place. A place
that will come to you at any moment
like a kitchen light. The window,
the curtains close as breath
drawn over the shadow couple, again,
again. They believe the sea cares
for them, truly it does. And at any moment
the sea will begin to break down
and weep.

Dogwalk Triptych

1. How Long

Sometimes a dog so much enjoys being
a dog, taking the shoe in his teeth,
tossing it toward the waves and when
the shoe makes a landing, possessing it
again, grounded between his paws,
his nose in its boat, all
despite the man's protests who retakes
the shoe and sits beside him, both
looking out to sea.

The man does not enjoy so much
being a man holding his shoe while
light shuffles the sea. Now is not
his time; it is the dog's time. Time being
only the eye of the observer
who travels at some other speed as waves
lift their flanks of silver light
and roll over to eternities. Named June.
A month

is nothing a dog knows. A second,
a day, a forty-minute nap, is all
the same. Aging is nothing—it's
the waiting that confounds him.
At home, once the door closes and the man
is gone, how long?
How long is how long?
The creature alone cannot measure duration.

But the sea is the sea was the sea is
the sea. And the man is watching it like a fire,
a great blue fire, bluer than memory
when it comes to him: the song,
an old song, song of the dogmen, *shu-wa,*

who want what they love to be
still a moment, *lu-la, lu-la,*
but it never is.

2. *Topos*

A man sits in his chair on the shore and opens his book.
The dog sits on the sand and looks up at the man.
This is geometry.
Soon the man is in a world of make-believe:
In the square, the cafes full of thieves,
political assassins. The dog, left behind,

smells something dead downwind,
a bird, a baby seal . . .
Geometry. Geography. Dogography.
All of it, a point and a point and the space
between. The book

is all about a man shipwrecked so long
he attains magical powers. Above the open
book an abandoned
boogie board passes, big slapstick on the light.
The dog settles his belly in the cool sand, chin
to the wind. The man turns a page.
The next wave holds up its hand in a trance
and then walks.

Orchestra, all of it. Things coming into
other things. The dog coming certain of
the scent. Its plot. Angle and dimension.
A beautiful girl in the book is drowned
while the man sleeps.

It's the middle, the exact middle for
all concerned, and would stay that way
except that the dog
loves the man more than the man loves the dog.
And a day at the sea is a date with memory.

3. Promenade

In the end, Blackie, all our names are
writ in water. Watch the shadows now
dress themselves and walk
the shore like dogs and men, like men
and long-legged birds. They are birds and
men and dogs in another time. Another

word for this: The dog
is running and turning running and turning
as the man heads back the way he came,
his shirtback blown out and luffing
big as bread. Full sail then, two
head for home. It's how the world
should end. But the man is thinking about
his toes, how one is beginning to cross with

another and the body's story is another:
The Greeks once thought the liver was the heart
and all passion resided there.
Now love lights in the hippocampus.
But love still lights. That's the main thing,

Blackie. A dog brain or a man brain,
it's all the same. Form ends and form
goes on: The dog

looking up though shadow's dug out
his eyes. Soon he'll put on his night ears, hear
through one wave after another,
tshu-ah, tshu-ah,
the high sirens calling this world

the other, insubstantial
but eternal, its beings unseizable mists.

About the Author

Beckian Fritz Goldberg is the author of three previous books of poetry, *Body Betrayer* (1991), *In the Badlands of Desire* (1993), and *Never Be the Horse* (1999). She teaches in the MFA Program at Arizona State University in Tempe.